ANIMAL KINGDOM CLASSIFICATION

CENTIPEDES, MILLIPEDES, SCORPIONS &

SPIDERS

By Daniel Gilpin
Content Adviser: Debbie Folkerts, Ph.D., Assistant Professor of
Biological Sciences, Auburn University, Alabama

Science Adviser: Terrence E. Young Jr., M.Ed., M.L.S.,
Jefferson Parish (Louisiana) Public School System

First published in the United States in 2006 by
Compass Point Books
3109 West 50th St., #115
Minneapolis, MN 55410

ANIMAL KINGDOM CLASSIFICATION—SPIDERS
was produced by

David West Children's Books
7 Princeton Court
55 Felsham Road
London SW15 1AZ

Designer: David West
Editors: Gail Bushnell, Nadia Higgins
Page Production: Les Tranby, James Mackey

Visit Compass Point Books on the Internet at
www.compasspointbooks.com
or e-mail your request to
custserv@compasspointbooks.com

Library of Congress Cataloging-in-Publication Data
Gilpin, Daniel.
    Centipedes, millipedes, scorpions, and spiders /
by Daniel Gilpin.
        p. cm.—(Animal kingdom classification)
Includes bibliographical references and index.
ISBN 0-7565-1254-9 (hardcover)
1. Arachnida—Juvenile literature. 2. Myriapoda—Juvenile literature. I. Title. II. Series.
QL452.2.G55 2006
595.6'2—dc22   2005008828

Front cover: Wolf spider
Opposite: Tarantula

ANIMAL KINGDOM CLASSIFICATION

CENTIPEDES, MILLIPEDES, SCORPIONS &
SPIDERS
Daniel Gilpin

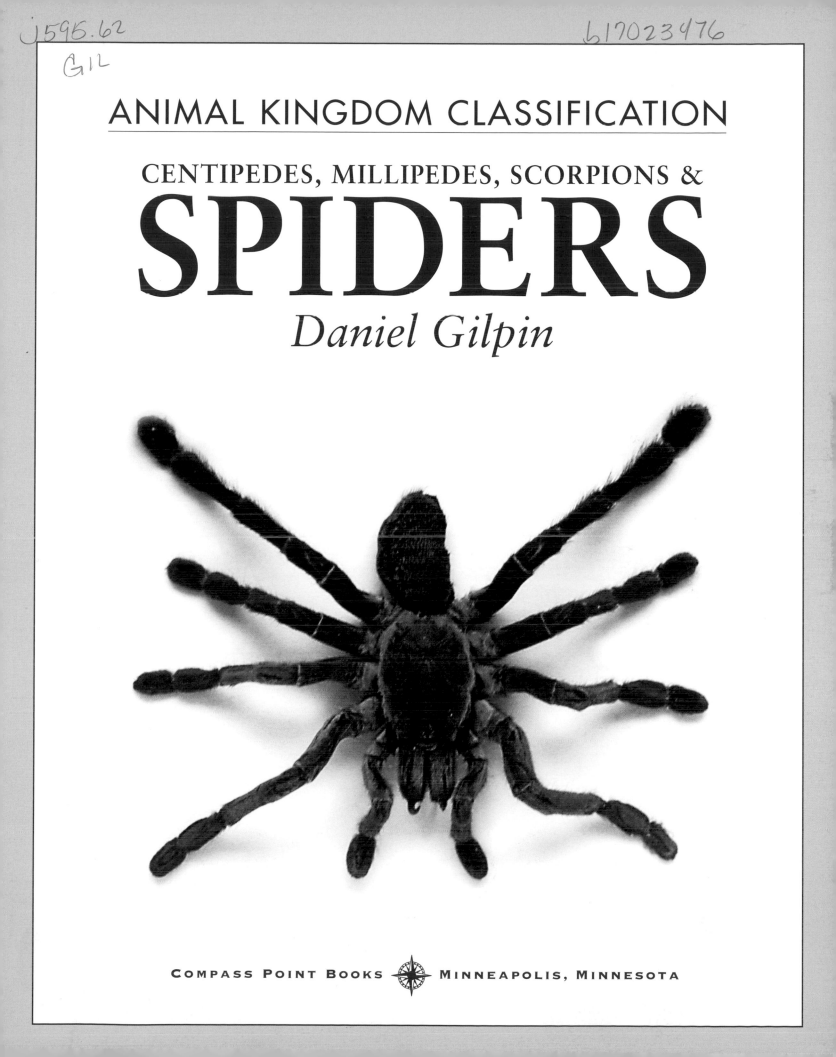

COMPASS POINT BOOKS ✦ MINNEAPOLIS, MINNESOTA

TABLE OF CONTENTS

INTRODUCTION

Spiders are everywhere. These eight-legged hunters are some of the most common creatures on Earth. Spiders are found from high mountain slopes to hot deserts, from dense forests to city streets. The only place spiders do not live is the sea.

Scientists classify, or sort, animals into different groups based on their shared characteristics. The six main groupings of animals, from the most general to the most specific, are: phylum, class, order, family, genus, and species. Spiders belong to the class of animals called arachnids. Other arachnids include mites, ticks, and scorpions.

Centipedes and millipedes belong to another animal class, called the myriapods. *Myriapod* means "many feet" in Latin. Both arachnids and myriapods are groups among the arthropods phylum, which includes all animals with exoskeletons and jointed legs.

GIANT CENTIPEDE

Most centipedes are active hunters, seeking out prey then killing it with venom injected through their hollow fangs. Only a few species are dangerous to people. Centipede means "100 feet." Most species have fewer feet than this, although some may have as many as 354.

EARLY LAND ANIMALS

Spiders, centipedes, and their relatives have been around for millions of years. In fact, these creatures were among the very first land animals. They were crawling over Earth before most modern creatures existed.

HOW DO WE KNOW?

Some animals become fossils after they die. Their tissues are slowly replaced by stone. Spiders, scorpions, and centipedes do not fossilize very well, but a few ancient ones have been preserved. The oldest of these date back more than 400 million years.

SET IN STONE

Amber (above) is a semiprecious stone made from fossilized sap. Some amber pieces contain animals that were trapped as the sap oozed from the tree. Though creatures are usually flattened in rock, those fossilized in amber keep their original shapes. This piece holds a spider that died millions of years ago.

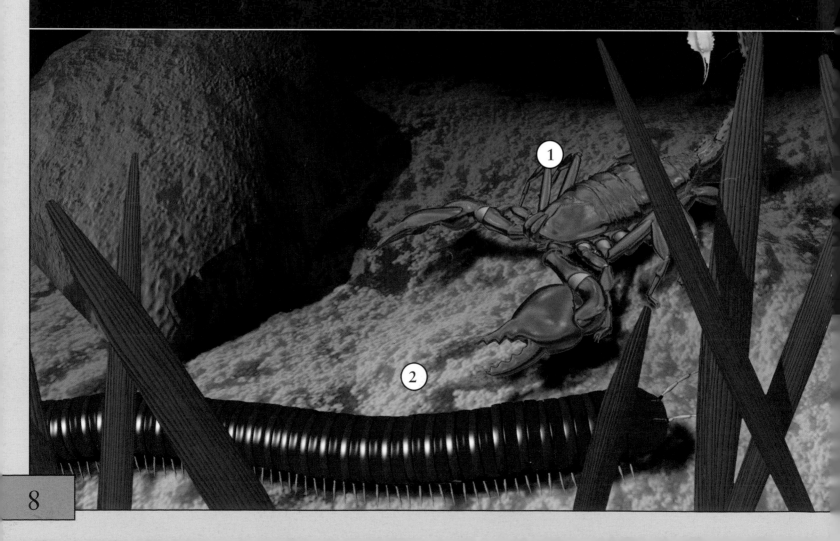

STABLE SHAPES

Arachnids and myriapods have been walking on Earth since before the dinosaurs existed. Incredibly, they have hardly changed, at least in terms of shape, in all of that time. Fossils show that early scorpions, like those around today, were hunting 410 million years ago, just after the first land plants appeared. Fossilized spiders, mites, centipedes, and millipedes have also been found that look almost exactly like those living today. Unlike in many other animals, the shape of arachnids and myriapods is successful today just as it was millions of years ago. Their lifestyles have remained almost unchanged over time.

EXTINCT GIANTS

The one thing that has changed since arachnids and myriapods first evolved is their size. Some early scorpions were much larger than any alive today. One, known only by its scientific name *Praearcturus gigas*, is thought to have grown up to 3.3 feet (1 meter) long. Some ancient millipedes were also gigantic, growing up to 6.6 feet (2 m) long and with bodies almost as thick as a man's thigh.

This illustration below shows arachnids and myriapods from the early Carboniferous Period, which began 360 million years ago. The creatures shown are: ❶ *the giant scorpion* Pulmonoscorpius; ❷ *the giant millipede* Arthropleura; ❸ *the giant centipede* Crussolum; ❹ *the spider* Attercopus; *and* ❺ *a Carboniferous sap-sucking mite.*

EIGHT-LEGGED HUNTERS

Arachnids come in many shapes and sizes. The most familiar arachnids are spiders, but this group includes several other types of animals, too.

DISTINCTIVE FEATURES

All arachnids have bodies divided into two parts. The front part is called the prosoma. It has two pairs of appendages, known as the chelicerae and pedipalps, and four pairs of legs. In some arachnids, such as scorpions, the pedipalps are shaped like pincers. The back part of the body is called its opisthosoma (or abdomen). The abdomen has no limbs but may extend into a tail-like structure, which sometimes carries a stinger.

HOW ARACHNIDS CAPTURE PREY

Almost all arachnids are carnivores, and most are hunters. Ticks are an exception, living as parasites on other animals. Scorpions, sun spiders, and many true spiders use speed to catch their prey. Scorpions and spiders then use venom to kill or disable their victims. Sun spiders simply crush prey with their massive jaws. Most whip spiders and whip scorpions kill prey by crushing it with their powerful hooked pedipalps.

Of course, not all spiders hunt by chasing prey. Many species make webs to trap their victims. Other spiders lie hidden, then ambush prey with surprise attacks. Some, such as trap-door spiders, even build their own hiding places.

Scorpion

Whip spider

Tick

Pseudoscorpion

Sun spider or wind scorpion

SEA SPIDERS

Sea spiders are not true spiders at all. They are not even arachnids. These odd animals belong to a group of their own, known as the pycnogonids. Unlike the arachnids, sea spiders can be found in all of the world's oceans. They eat soft-bodied invertebrates, such as sponges and sea anemones, sucking up the tissue of their prey through a long tubelike mouth, or proboscis. Sea spiders' legspans range in size from less than 0.04 inches (1 millimeter) to more than 20 inches (50.8 centimeters). Most have four pairs of legs, although some may have up to seven.

Sea spider on a sponge

SPIDER BODIES

Most people would recognize a spider if they saw one. But what exactly are the characteristics that set spiders apart from other animals? Like other arachnids, spiders have eight legs, but they also have fangs, which deliver venom, and special glands to produce silk.

TWO HALVES

A spider's body is divided into two parts, separated by a narrow waist. The front part, known as the prosoma, contains the stomach and brain. The rear part, known as the opisthosoma, or abdomen, contains important internal organs like the silk glands. Considering its thickness, spider's silk is stronger than steel.

SPIDER'S WEB

Spiders are the only animals to make webs. Some species construct orb webs (above), which they use to catch flying insects. The spiraling strands of silk are covered with sticky liquid. As it struggles to escape, trapped prey becomes more and more entangled in the web.

HEART

The heart pumps blood around the body. Large spiders' hearts beat up to 70 times a minute, while those of smaller species beat up to 200 times a minute.

EGGS

After mating, the eggs develop in the female's abdomen. Once they have reached a certain size, they are laid and mature further before hatching.

Spinnerets

SILK GLANDS

These make silk from various proteins. The silk is drawn out from the glands and spun by fingerlike appendages called spinnerets (above).

Side view of book lung

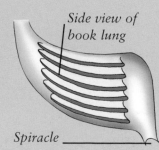

Spiracle

BOOK LUNGS

These are formed from plates of tissue, which transfer oxygen from the air into the blood. Spiders' blood is usually blue.

BRAIN

The brain is linked to a large bunch of nerve cells called the ganglion. Nerve fibers run from the brain and ganglion throughout the body.

PEDIPALPS

These paired leglike limbs are used as feelers to help the spider find its way around in the dark and to manipulate food.

FANGS

A spider's fangs inject venom into its prey. Most spiders have fangs that swing inward from the side (1), allowing them to hold on to their prey. Some larger spiders, such as tarantulas, have fangs that stab directly downward (2), pinning their victims to the ground.

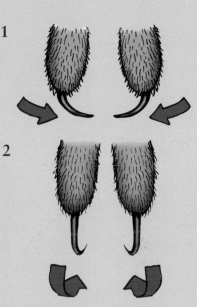

1

2

EYES

The central pair of eyes face forward to help the spider judge distances. Most spiders have eight eyes, although some have as many as 12, and others don't have any.

SUCKING STOMACH

Spiders' venom contains digestive juices, which break down prey into a liquefied soup. The spider uses powerful muscles to expand its stomach and create a suction force, which draws the "soup" in through its mouth.

BODY PARTS

All spiders have four pairs of legs, although in some, the pedipalps are so long that they look almost like a fifth pair. The two body sections separate spiders from insects, which have three: the head, thorax, and abdomen.

Legs (8)

Opisthosoma (1)

Prosoma (1)

Fangs (2)

Pedipalps (2)

SPIDER GALLERY

Although spiders all have certain features in common, they are actually surprisingly varied, especially when looked at closely.

PHYSICAL DIFFERENCES

More than 30,000 species of spiders are known to exist on Earth today, and there are probably many more that have yet to be discovered. These creatures come in a huge range of shapes, sizes, and colors. The smallest, the Patu Marple spider of Samoa, has a legspan of less than 0.02 inches (0.5 mm). The largest, the Goliath bird-eating spider, has legs that could reach either side of a dinner plate. Even within species, there are major differences. Female spiders are almost always much larger than males, and the colors of the two sexes are often very different.

STRANGE BEHAVIOR

As well as looking different, spiders hunt and behave in different ways. Some hide motionless for hours waiting for prey to come along, while others sit at the centers of intricate webs. Still more wander in search of victims to chase down, overpower, and kill.

Although spiders are hunters, they often find themselves on the menus of other creatures. Some go to extraordinary lengths to escape. The wheel spider of Africa's Namib Desert literally rolls down the sand dunes, folding up its legs to make its body into a perfect ball.

ARANEAE

These pictures give some idea of the variety there is in the spider order, Araneae. Jumping spiders ❶ are small, compact hunters with incredible eyesight, while daddy-longleg spiders ❷ move slowly on spindly limbs. Most crab spiders ❸ lie in wait for prey among the petals of flowers. The water spider ❹ hunts among the plants in lakes and ponds, while carrying its own bubble of air. Tarantulas ❺ are large, active predators that travel in search of a meal. Orb-web spiders ❻ wait for their food to come to them, while wolf spiders ❼ have long, sturdy legs to outrun their prey. Other groups include the dwarf spiders, spitting spiders, comb-footed spiders, funnel weavers, fishing spiders, and huntsmen. All of these have their own distinctive body shapes and forms of behavior. Many are shown elsewhere in this book.

WEBS

Spiders are nature's master builders. Their webs are among the most complex and intricate structures built by any species.

FISHING FOR INSECTS

In many ways, a spider's web is like a fishing net. The main difference is that it catches creatures moving through air rather than water. Most spiders string their webs between the stems and branches of plants. They then sit and wait, often at the center of the web, for insects to accidentally fly into it.

Most spiders' webs are covered with sticky material to hold flying prey. Any insect unfortunate enough to fly into the web is stuck fast. As it struggles to escape, the insect causes vibrations in the web, which alert the spider to its presence.

TYPES OF WEBS

The most familiar type of web is the flat orb web. Not all spiders build these, however. Some make three-dimensional webs (main) instead. Orb webs are often hard to see. Some spiders add more visible sections (right) to stop birds from flying into them.

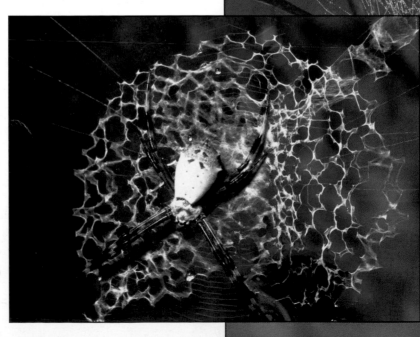

16

*Trap-door spiders (below) build silk
tubes with hinged lids, where they lie
in wait for prey. Other species make
retreats for resting, like this bird-eating
spider inside a bamboo stem (right).*

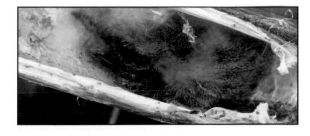

NET CASTER

The ogre-faced
spider hangs
above a leaf
or branch and
waits for a
victim to come
into range.
Then the
spider casts
a fuzzy trap
over its
unsuspecting
prey.

Ogre-faced spider

MAKING A WEB

An orb-web spider begins by releasing
a thread of silk that blows in the wind.
When this thread hits something, it
sticks to it. The spider travels along
this bridge, adding extra lines to
strengthen it. The spider then makes
two loose threads to hang from the
bridge. It links the two together and
continues to spin downward until it
hits something. The Y-shaped structure
forms the frame. Spokes are then added
before a long, spiraling thread is run
from the edge to the center.

HUNTING

Spiders are carnivores that capture live prey. Most live on a diet of insects, but some of the larger species hunt and kill small vertebrates, such as mice and lizards. Different spiders hunt in different ways. Some make webs or lie in wait, but others are more active.

SPEED

Some spiders catch their prey simply by outrunning it. Most wolf spiders hunt in this way, chasing prey over flat ground or through the branches of trees. Other speedy hunters include North America's hobo spider and the larger European house spiders. One of the latter, *Tegenaria gigantea,* is widely acknowledged as the world's fastest spider, reaching speeds of up to 1.2 miles (1.9 kilometers) per hour.

STEALTH

Tarantulas and many other large spiders hunt by stealth, creeping up on their victims unnoticed until they are close enough to strike. Stealth is a technique sometimes used by smaller spiders, too, particularly when attacking insects that can fly. Wolf spiders and other species that would normally rely on speed revert to stealth when trying to catch butterflies or other winged prey.

RAFT SPIDER

Raft spiders hunt on lakes and ponds, using the water's surface like a giant web (left). When an insect lands on the water, it creates ripples on the surface, which the spider detects. Raft spiders have specially adapted feet that allow them to walk on water. Each foot is covered with water-resistant hairs that help spread the spider's weight.

SPITTING SPIDER

The spitting spider has a very unusual method of hunting. It spits poisonous silk over its prey. Unlike other spiders, the spitting spider has silk glands in the front part of its body, the prosoma, which create the silk it uses to immobilize its victims. The spitting spider hunts at night and usually fires its silk from less than 0.4 inches (1 cm) away.

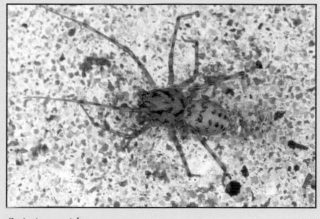

Spitting spider

SURPRISE

Catching prey off guard saves valuable energy that would be used up by chasing it. Some spiders achieve the element of surprise by using camouflage. Others create their own disguises. One desert species makes a small silk net that it covers with sand and hides underneath.

Another way to catch prey is to appear so quickly that the victim cannot react. Jumping spiders do this, landing on victims before they even know they are being attacked. Jumping spiders can make accurate leaps 60 times their own body length. That is like a lion jumping on you from 130 yards (118 m) away.

JUMPING SPIDERS

These hunters catch prey by surprise. Jumping spiders have much better eyesight than most others. This lets the spider not only spot prey, but also work out exactly how far away it is before leaping in for the attack.

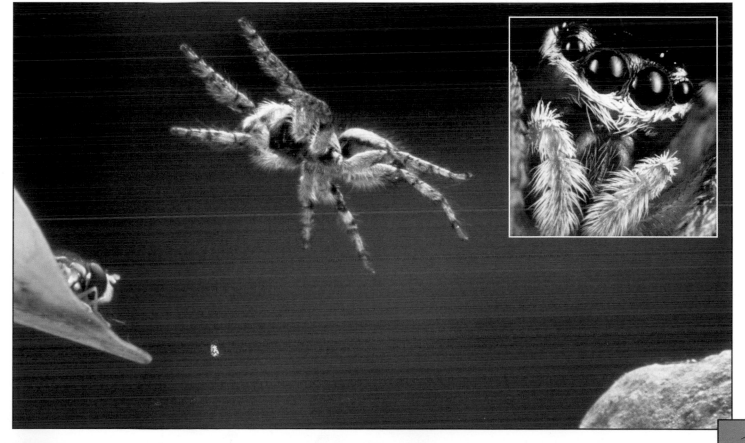

BIG AND FEARSOME

Giant spiders are some people's worst nightmare. Other people keep these formidable creatures as pets.

WHERE THEY LIVE
The world's largest spiders live wild in the tropics. Tarantulas and their relatives are found in hot parts of North America, South America, Africa, and Asia. Despite their size, few are deadly to humans, but all can give a vicious bite if provoked. The Goliath bird-eating spider from South America is the biggest of all. Its body can be 3.5 inches (9 cm) long.

BABOON SPIDER

Baboon spiders are Africa's version of the tarantula. Unlike most tarantulas, they rarely emerge from their burrows, but hide in them to wait for prey.

TARANTULAS

The name tarantula was originally used for just a single species of wolf spider from southern Europe, Lycosa tarentula. Today, it is also used as a general name for a variety of large tropical American and Asian spiders.

MEXICAN RED-KNEED TARANTULA

This large spider lives in deserts and dry scrubland from western Mexico to northern South America. It feeds on large insects and small vertebrates such as lizards. The Mexican red-kneed tarantula spends the day hidden in its burrow and only emerges to hunt at night.

ROSE BIRD-EATING SPIDER

Bird-eating spiders include the largest spiders of all. These giants live in tropical South America, where they hunt a wide variety of small animals, including the occasional roosting bird. When threatened, bird-eating spiders produce a hissing sound by rubbing their bristly legs together. Compared to other large spiders, bird-eating spiders can run quickly.

ATTACK AND DEFENSE

Most tarantulas and other large spiders hunt at night, when their prey is less active. They find the creatures they feed on by touch, using their pedipalps to locate victims. A few species set silk "trip wires" around themselves. The trip wires are triggered when prey crosses over them, and the spider attacks.

Tarantulas use venom to kill prey. They also bite as a last resort when defending themselves. If threatened, they rear up to appear bigger. They also shed hairs, which irritate their attacker's eyes and nose.

SPIDER PETS

Tarantulas make surprisingly good pets. The bites of most species are painful but not life-threatening, and tarantulas won't bite at all if handled properly. Looking after tarantulas requires special equipment. These spiders need to be kept warm at all times. Most tarantula enthusiasts keep their pets in glass tanks with secure lids. A dish of water is left inside the tank to keep the air humid.

Pet tarantula

FEEDING AND POISON

Spiders have powerful fangs but no real teeth. To eat their prey, they have to turn its tissues into liquid, which they can then suck into their bodies.

KILLING BITE

A spider's fangs are sharp, pointed tubes, which are used for injecting venom into its prey. This venom quickly immobilizes victims, preventing them from fighting back and possibly injuring the spider.

Spider's venom works in one of two main ways. Some spiders produce venom that affects the brain and nervous system, causing muscle cramps that quickly lead to complete paralysis. Others produce venom that destroys the victim's muscles. This type of venom acts more slowly, so the spider has to grip its prey tightly while the poison takes effect.

UNEVEN CONTEST

Some spiders will tackle prey much larger than themselves. Although this might seem dangerous, these spiders have an unfair advantage—their venom. Most spiders that take on bigger animals produce fast-acting nerve toxins. One bite renders their opponents helpless as their muscles seize up, leaving them unable to move.

FIRM GRIP

Most large spiders, such as tarantulas (inset) and baboon spiders (left), have huge, downward-pointing fangs. These deliver a fatal dose of venom and also hold prey captive, pinning it to the ground. These spiders are surprisingly strong. Their long fangs are slightly curved, which helps them to grip struggling victims.

SLOW DIGESTION

As well as killing prey, spider's venom slowly breaks down its tissues. Spiders cannot chew their food. Instead, they feed by sucking in their victim's liquefied flesh. Any lumps or particles are filtered out by tiny hairs in and around the spider's mouth.

Once it is inside the spider's body, the soupy liquid is broken down further. Slowly, it is transferred from the sucking stomach (in the prosoma) to the midgut (in the abdomen). Here, basic nutritious substances are absorbed into the blood.

HUMAN CASUALTIES

Some spiders produce venom that is dangerous to humans. Redbacks, black widows, and Sydney funnel-web spiders all have potentially fatal bites. Fortunately, antivenom is available to counteract the venom of all of these species.

One of the most dangerous spiders is the Brazilian huntsman. It is not only deadly poisonous but is also very aggressive. It frequently comes into contact with people in its native Brazil, hiding among clothes and furniture.

SPIDER'S PANTRY

Many web-spinning spiders store captured prey to eat later. Once they have paralyzed or killed their victim, they wrap it up in a silk cocoon and hang it safely nearby to be eaten when fresh food is scarce.

DEADLY WIDOW

The black widow is North America's most dangerous spider. Its venom is extremely powerful and has been known to kill humans. Female black widows are much larger and more dangerous than the males. Even so, these spiders are surprisingly small— the body of a female black widow is not much bigger than a pea. Black widows are web spinners that like dry, dark places. This sometimes brings them into contact with humans, particularly in sheds and garages.

A black widow shows the red hourglass markings on its abdomen. This lets attackers know that it is poisonous.

CAMOUFLAGE AND DEFENSE

Camouflage helps spiders stay out of trouble. It also helps them catch prey. Not all spiders are camouflaged. Some have other methods of defense.

DISAPPEARING ACTS

Spiders use camouflage to blend in with their surroundings. By matching the colors and patterns on their bodies to those of their habitat, they effectively disappear into the background. Camouflage is especially important for ambush hunters, which rely on prey straying close enough for them to make a sudden attack.

A few spiders use other ways to avoid being seen. Trap-door spiders, for instance, dig burrows in which to hide from prey.

BLURRED OUTLINE

When they feel threatened, daddy-longleg spiders vibrate their webs rapidly. This behavior helps them avoid being eaten. By shaking from side to side in this way, a spider can blur the outline of its body, making it harder for a predator to spot and capture it.

PERFECT MATCH

Crab spiders include some of the best camouflaged spiders of all. Many of these ambush hunters match the petals of the flowers in which they wait for prey. Crab spiders are highly territorial, and only one will inhabit a flower at a time. Some species can slowly change their color to match new surroundings.

MIMICRY

One way to avoid predators is to look like something inedible. In Malaysia, there is a crab spider that imitates bird droppings. Its "costume" comes complete with splash marks, fashioned from silk. Other spiders mimic objects like leaves and twigs.

Some spiders rely on speed to escape predators. One species, *Sunpunna picta*, combines speed with an ingenious disguise. While it runs, it waves its front legs like a wasp's antennae, confusing its attacker and frightening it away.

TWO FORMS OF DEFENSE

Some spiders (inset) mimic ants and live among them to hide from predators. Others have defensive weapons. The spiny-backed orb weaver has large spikes that make it unpleasant to eat.

SPIDER ENEMIES

Many types of birds feed on spiders. Other predators include lizards and small mammals such as mice. Some wasps lay their eggs in spiders' bodies, paralyzing their prey. The wasps use the spiders as a living food supply for their growing larvae.

Wasp attacking a spider

BACK OFF!

Tarantulas rear up and stretch out their front legs to make themselves look bigger when they are attacked. This behavior also helps large animals see them and so avoid stepping on them.

COURTSHIP AND BABIES

Most spiders live solitary lives and only come together to breed. Female spiders make dangerous mates but can be attentive mothers.

FINDING A PARTNER

Many spiders have particular breeding seasons. At certain times of the year, usually in spring or summer, male spiders leave their webs or burrows and go roaming in search of females. Some male spiders seem to wander aimlessly until they meet a female, but others follow particular clues. Some female spiders produce smelly chemicals called pheromones, for example, which males of the same species recognize and use to track down females.

Once he has found a female, the male spider approaches carefully. Male spiders are usually smaller than females and have to make sure they have been recognized before they get too close. Most send some kind of signal to identify themselves, so they are not mistaken for prey.

WEB SIGNALS
Mating is a risky business for male spiders. The males of many web-spinning species, like this orb weaver, pluck the strands of a female's web in a certain way. This lets the owner know exactly who's approaching.

MATING DANCES

Male jumping spiders perform courtship dances to calm females and signal their intention to mate. Different species have different dances, but most involve the male waving his front legs in a certain way while directly in front of the female.

Male jumping spider signaling

PROTECTIVE PARENT
Female wolf spiders carry their egg sacs around with them. When the young hatch, they crawl up on to their mother's back for protection, clinging to special knob-shaped hairs.

GROWING EGGS
Once a male and female spider have mated, the two usually part, with the male backing slowly away. Occasionally, the female will attack and kill her partner.

The fertilized eggs develop for a few days or weeks inside the female's body before she lays them. Most spiders protect their newly laid eggs by weaving special sacs of silk around them. Some species then carry these sacs or stand guard over them until their young hatch. Others simply hide the sacs and abandon them.

HATCHING AND MOLTING
Young spiders (above) hatch as miniature versions of their parents, able to feed themselves. As they grow, they molt, or break out of their skins, leaving behind the shed exoskeletons that once covered their bodies (right).

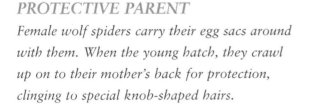

SCORPION BODIES

View from underneath

Like spiders, scorpions are arachnids. Although their bodies look quite different, they actually have a lot of features in common. All scorpions have eight legs, for example. They also breathe using book lungs.

DIFFERENT SECTIONS

A scorpion's body is divided into two main sections, the prosoma and the opisthosoma. The prosoma contains the mouthparts and has the legs and pedipalps attached to it. Its top surface is covered by a single, solid plate called the carapace. The opisthosoma is split into several segments. The segments at the end form a flexible tail-like structure, which carries a venom-filled stinger. A scorpion's pedipalps are shaped like pincers and used for grasping prey. As a whole, the body is largely flattened, enabling scorpions to squeeze into surprisingly small spaces.

PECTINES

These comblike sensory organs are unique to scorpions. Their exact function is not properly understood, but they are thought to be used during mating, possibly to detect pheromones.

PEDIPALPS

These appendages end in powerful pincers for grabbing prey and holding it while feeding. Like the legs, the pedipalps are jointed, allowing them to be moved into almost any position.

BODY PARTS

Scorpions are easily identified by their overall shape and poisonous sting. The body is split into 13 segments, making it quite flexible. Unlike in spiders, the prosoma and opisthosoma merge together, and most of the body is encased by tough plates of tissue.

Prosoma (1 segment)

Opisthosoma (12 segments)

Legs (8)

Eyes (up to 10)

Pedipalps (2)

MOUTHPARTS

These are used mainly for feeding and grooming. A few species can rub their mouthparts together to make a hissing sound that warns large animals to stay away.

STINGER

The scorpion's stinger is its most potent weapon and is mainly used to kill or disable prey. The venom of most species affects the nervous system, paralyzing victims before killing them. The stinger can be moved into almost any position very quickly.

EYES

Most scorpions have eight eyes, although some have six, others 10, and a few have none at all. The eyes are relatively simple and can only focus on prey at ranges of an inch or less.

HEART

The tubular heart runs along much of the length of the body. Each time it beats, blood is forced from both ends. Scorpions' blood is colorless.

LEGS

The long legs have flexible joints, enabling the scorpion to scuttle quickly over rough terrain.

BOOK LUNGS

Like the book lungs of spiders, these are made up of stacks of thin plates of tissue. As air is drawn into the book lungs, oxygen passes through the outer membranes of the plates and into the surrounding blood.

BRAIN

The brain is made up of two bunches of nerve tissue, known as ganglia. A long nerve cord runs from the brain and along the body. Shorter nerve cords branch off into the limbs.

STOMACH

The stomach expands to suck in liquid food. Scorpions feed mostly on the body fluids of their prey. Small pieces of tissue, broken off with the pincers and mouthparts, are dissolved in a cavity behind the mouth before swallowing.

Scorpion Behavior

S corpions are found in most hot countries. For their size, they are impressive predators, often tackling prey larger than themselves.

HABITATS AND HUNTING

Scorpions are true survivors. Many species live in deserts, and all can cope with extremes of heat and cold. Experiments have shown that scorpions can survive being frozen solid in ice, although they need warmth to remain active enough to hunt.

Most scorpions spend the daylight hours resting under rocks or in other natural crevices and only emerge to feed at night. Their eyesight is poor, so they find most of their prey by touch. They are active hunters, wandering widely in search of victims. Once prey is located, scorpions attack with frightening ferocity and speed.

BUTHID

Scorpions are usually classified into eight families. The largest family, Buthidae, has more than 500 species. Most buthid scorpions have thick tails. Buthids kill most of their prey with venom rather than their pincers.

MATERNAL CARE

Scorpions give birth to live young. The females carry their babies around on their backs until the babies are large enough to fend for themselves.

SCORPIONID

The large Scorpionidae family of scorpions contains more than 200 species and includes the biggest scorpions. Most scorpionids kill prey with their pincers and only use their stingers for defense.

SCORPIONS ON THE ATTACK

Most scorpions deal with prey in one of two ways. Insects and other small creatures are usually grasped in the pincers and crushed to death or eaten alive. Larger animals are grabbed then subdued with a sting. Once injected, the venom acts quickly to stop prey from struggling and soon kills it outright.

Some scorpions are dangerous to humans. Mexico has many deadly species, and more than 1,000 people are killed by scorpions there every year. The most dangerous scorpions are those with small pincers and large tails because they inject the greatest quantities of venom.

FEEDING AND DEFENSE

Scorpions suck the juices from their prey (inset) and discard most of the solid matter. When threatened, a scorpion adopts a distinctive pose (below), spreading its pincers wide and arching its back to display its stinger. If this fails to frighten off its enemy, the scorpion attacks, jabbing quickly with its tail as it tries to inject a dose of venom.

MINI-SCORPIONS

Some arachnids look like spiders or scorpions but are neither. These creatures are classified by scientists into their own distinct groups.

TEN ORDERS

Altogether, there are 10 different orders of arachnids. Spiders and scorpions make up two of them, and daddy longlegs a third. Two other orders contain less well-known creatures such as sun spiders (order Solifugae) and mites and ticks (order Acarina). Most arachnid orders are nonvenomous.

TYPES OF MINI-SCORPIONS

Mini-scorpions is a catchall name for the five remaining orders of arachnids: whip spiders, whip scorpions, micro-whip scorpions, pseudoscorpions, and ricinuleids. Micro-whip scorpions are the smallest of these, measuring 0.08 inches (2 mm) long. They inhabit soil and hunt the tiny animals that live among its particles. Ricinuleids are slightly larger and live in fallen leaves.

WHIP SCORPION

These creatures are named for the long, bristlelike structure on the end of the abdomen. A gland at the base of the whip produces acid that is sprayed at attackers.

PSEUDOSCORPION

Like true scorpions, these little creatures have powerful pincers, although they lack a stinging tail. Pseudoscorpions have their venom glands in their pincers and poison prey as soon as they grab it.

GIANT WHIP SCORPION

The largest whip scorpion, this North American species grows up to 3 inches (8 cm) long. Whip scorpions hunt at night for insects and small prey, using their long front legs as feelers.

LITTLE HUNTERS

Only a few species of micro-whip scorpions and ricinuleids have been discovered. Their small size and unusual habitats make them rarely seen. Scientists believe that many more species exist but are still undiscovered. Pseudoscorpions are better understood. They too are small—the largest are less than 0.3 inches (8 mm) long—but they come into contact with humans more often. Pseudoscorpions occur in a wide variety of habitats. Some even live in people's homes.

WHIP SPIDER

These arachnids are similar to whip scorpions but lack the bristlelike tail. The "whips" of a whip spider are formed by its extremely long front legs.

PIGGYBACK RIDE

Like many other arachnids, whip spiders carry their young on their backs until the babies reach their first molt.

SUN SPIDERS

Sun spiders are the cheetahs of the invertebrate world. These long-legged hunters catch prey by speed, then crush it with their massive mouthparts.

SOLIFUGIDS

Sun spiders are not true spiders at all but belong to their own order, Solifugae. Their other common names include camel spiders, Romans, beard cutters, and wind scorpions. Most scientists simply call them solifugids to avoid confusion.

Sun spiders range from around 1 inch (2.5 cm) to 6 inches (15 cm) in size. The smaller species are active by day, but most larger sun spiders only come out to hunt at night. Prey includes spiders, scorpions, insects, and small vertebrates. Sun spiders are also cannibalistic, killing their own kind if other prey is unavailable.

WHERE THEY LIVE

Sun spiders are mainly desert animals. With their wide, open spaces, deserts suit the sun spider's method of hunting, leaving fleeing prey animals nowhere to hide.

Top view of sun spider

BIG APPETITE

Food is scarce in the desert, so when a sun spider finds a meal, it feeds until it is almost ready to burst. Sun spiders are not fussy eaters and will also eat leftover food from the kills of other predators.

Under view of sun spider

ESCAPE ARTIST

Sun spiders are fast runners, but they have an even faster way of moving to get away from predators. When threatened in deserts, some sun spiders curl into a ball. They then roll down a sand dune, gathering speed as they go. If this fails to shake off a predator, the sun spider tries its next trick—burrowing into the sand to escape.

Sun spider rolling away from danger

BODY FEATURES

A sun spider's most impressive feature is its huge mouthparts (right). These arachnids appear to have 10 legs (above), but in fact, they have eight. The front pair of "legs" are the pedipalps, which are sensitive to touch. Small, racket-shaped organs are attached to the first segments of their last pair of legs. The function of these is not known, although they probably play a role in mating.

RECORD BREAKERS

Sun spiders can run at up to 10 miles (16 km) per hour, making them the fastest land invertebrates. These creatures hold another record: They deliver the strongest bite for their body size of any animal. Sun spiders' mouthparts are absolutely huge. In fact, they are the largest of any land-living invertebrate. These mouthparts grab prey and crush it to death, allowing the sun spider to feed at its leisure.

TINY TICKS, MIGHTY MITES

Ticks and mites include some of the world's smallest animals. Many of these creatures live as parasites on the bodies of other animals.

THE ACARINA ORDER

Ticks and mites belong to the order Acarina. Compared to other arachnids, they have unusually large abdomens. Another distinctive feature is the capitulum, a sort of false head, set apart from the rest of the body. Adult ticks and mites have eight legs like other arachnids, but their larvae usually have six. Most ticks and mites are small, and some are microscopic.

TICKS

All ticks are parasites that feed on the blood of mammals, birds, and reptiles. Most find their hosts by waiting in grass or other vegetation, sometimes for weeks or even months. When a suitable animal passes, they climb aboard, gripping on with their sharp claws.

Ticks feed using a sharp, hollow part called a hypostome. This is stabbed into the host's skin and used for sucking up blood. The hypostome has backward-pointing barbs to keep it in place.

BROWN TICK ON A DOG

A tick's abdomen enlarges as it fills with blood. Some ticks may expand to more than 200 times their original size. Ticks secrete a cementlike substance that glues them to their host.

SAND TAMPAN

This tick lives in dry and semidesert habitats, from southern Africa to India and Sri Lanka. It feeds on the blood of mammals, including humans, and is a serious pest of livestock, sometimes transmitting disease.

RED VELVET MITE

The red velvet mite is one of the largest of all mites. The adult mite is an active predator, while the larvae are parasitic. They ride around on insects and other invertebrates, feeding on their hosts' body juices.

MITES

Mites are generally much smaller than ticks, which range in size. Some ticks are smaller than a sesame seed, while others may be as large as a fingernail. The largest mites are about the same size as the smallest ticks, up to 0.1 inches (3 mm) long. The smallest are microscopic.

Unlike ticks, mites have evolved to feed on a wide range of foods. A few are parasites, but many more are active hunters. Some feed on the juices of plants, and others eat discarded pieces of animal tissue. Dust mites live in our homes in huge numbers. As their name suggests, they feed on house dust, which is made from tiny particles of shed human skin.

PARASITIC KILLER

Some mites live together as parasites on an insect, feeding on their host's vital juices. A large number of mites can eventually kill the host. The mites then seek out a new insect. Some parasitic mites specialize in attacking social insects such as bees. The fact that their hosts live together is an advantage. If the one they are feeding on dies, there are usually other hosts not far away.

Parasitellus focurum
mites on a bumble bee

HORSESHOE CRABS

Horseshoe crabs are not real crabs at all. Crabs are crustaceans, like lobsters. Horseshoe crabs have their own class among the arthropods.

OCEAN DWELLERS

Unlike arachnids, which live on land, horseshoe crabs spend most of their lives in the sea. These primitive invertebrates only emerge from the water at certain times of the year to spawn, meeting in huge numbers to lay their eggs.

Horseshoe crabs live mainly in warm seas. Today, there are just five species, although many more existed in the past.

BODY PARTS

It's no wonder horseshoe crabs look prehistoric. These creatures have hardly changed since they first appeared more than 400 million years ago.

A horseshoe crab has six pairs of appendages, of which four pairs are walking legs. On land, these help the animal shuffle along. In the sea, they are used for swimming and for pushing water over the gills to help the horseshoe crab take up oxygen. A horseshoe crab's gills are similar to the book lungs of arachnids, leading some scientists to suggest that the two classes might be related. Horseshoe crabs eat seaweed and small animals such as worms. Their mouth is a slit between their "legs."

APTLY NAMED

Horseshoe crabs are known as such because of their distinctive shape. Their bodies are covered with a tough outer shell, hinged in the middle to make movement easier.

BEACH INVASION

Most horseshoe crabs spawn in late spring or early summer. They lay their eggs during evening high tides when the moon is full. The eggs develop and hatch in the sand, and the babies enter the sea with the next high tide at full moon.

MYRIAPODS

Centipedes and millipedes have more legs than any other type of animal. Centipedes are active predators that hunt down small prey. Millipedes are herbivores, feeding on leaves and other plant matter.

TELLING THEM APART

At first glance, centipedes and millipedes look very similar, but a closer look reveals differences that set them apart. The main difference is the way their legs are arranged. A centipede has one pair of legs for every segment of its body. A millipede has two pairs for each segment. This would suggest that millipedes have more legs than centipedes, and that is usually true. Centipedes have between 30 and 354 legs, depending on the species. Millipedes have between 24 and 750. The way the legs emerge from the body is another good way to tell centipedes and millipedes apart. The legs of centipedes are usually long and stick out from the sides of the body, allowing for large strides and fast movement. Millipedes have shorter legs, which they usually keep underneath their bodies.

CENTIPEDE

Centipedes have flat bodies made up of many segments. Some species shed legs when attacked. These legs continue to move and distract predators while the centipede escapes.

FINDING FOOD

Centipedes hunt other creatures. They kill prey with venom injected through hollow fangs. Most centipedes have flat bodies, allowing them to follow prey almost anywhere. They are also quick, capable of outrunning most prey.

Millipedes move much more slowly than centipedes, partly because their food does not try to escape. In fact, most millipedes live surrounded by an almost endless supply of food—the fallen leaves on forest floors.

MILLIPEDE
Millipedes have
rounded bodies covered
with tough exoskeletons. This
makes it hard for the fangs of spiders
or other small predators to get a grip. Most
millipedes give off a smelly, brown liquid when
attacked, which keeps most larger animals away.

MYRIAPODS IN ACTION

Centipedes and millipedes behave in different ways. The way they act is affected mainly by their surroundings, predators, and choice of food.

HABITATS

Myriapods are restricted to damp habitats. Unlike most other land arthropods, their exoskeletons lack a waxy layer, and their bodies quickly lose water in dry surroundings. Most millipedes live by bulldozing their way through fallen leaves. Centipedes are found in a wider variety of habitats. Some live on forest floors, some in caves, and some in soil. Soil-dwelling species have long, slender bodies and move through the dirt almost like worms.

HAIRY MARY

Centipedes have poor eyesight and many, including the house centipede or "Hairy Mary" (above), hunt at night. They find prey by touch, using long antennae. Some use the last pair of legs like feelers when moving backward.

CREATING COMPOST

Millipedes play a vital role in forest ecosystems. They help break down dead plant matter and turn it into soil.

LITTLE AND LARGE

Millipedes vary greatly in size. The smallest may be less than 0.1 inches (3 mm) long. The largest, the African giant millipede (inset), can reach 11 inches (28 cm). Most millipedes, such as the one in the main picture above, grow to just an inch or so length.

MYRIAPOD MOVEMENT

Centipedes survive by actively seeking out prey. Their long legs make them speedy hunters—the fastest can reach nearly 1.2 miles (2 km) per hour in short bursts. The legs of centipedes move alternately: When a leg on one side of a segment goes forward, the other goes back, so the animal moves along with a wriggling motion. Millipedes move all four legs on a segment together. This allows them to move forward without wriggling their bodies at all.

PILL MILLIPEDES

These creatures are shorter than most other millipedes and behave differently when under attack. Instead of squirting foul-smelling fluid, they roll into a ball. This protects their legs and softer, more vulnerable underparts, leaving nothing for a predator to grab. Like all millipedes, pill millipedes have a chalky substance in their exoskeleton to strengthen it.

43

ANIMAL CLASSIFICATION

The animal kingdom can be split into two main groups, vertebrates (with a backbone) and invertebrates (without a backbone). From these two main groups, scientists classify, or sort, animals further based on their shared characteristics.

The six main groupings of animals, from the most general to the most specific, are: phylum, class, order, family, genus, and species. This system was created by Carolus Linnaeus.

To see how this system works, follow the example of how human beings are classified in the vertebrate group and how earthworms are classified in the invertebrate group.

ANIMAL KINGDOM

VERTEBRATE	INVERTEBRATE
PHYLUM: Chordates	**PHYLUM:** Annelida
CLASS: Mammals	**CLASS:** Oligochaeta
ORDER: Primates	**ORDER:** Haplotaxida
FAMILY: Hominids	**FAMILY:** Lumbricidae
GENUS: *Homo*	**GENUS:** *Lumbricus*
SPECIES: *sapiens*	**SPECIES:** *terrestris*

There are more than 30 groups of phyla. The nine most common are listed below along with their common name.

Annelida
(SEGMENTED WORMS)

ARTHROPODA
(ARTHROPODS)

Chordata
(CHORDATES)

Cnidaria
(CNIDARIANS)

Echinodermata
(ECHINODERMS)

Mollusca
(MOLLUSKS)

Nematoda
(ROUNDWORMS)

Platyhelminthes
(FLATWORMS)

Porifera
(SPONGES)

This book highlights animals from the Arthorpods phylum. Follow the example below to learn how scientists classify the *coloradensis*, or thin-legged wolf spider.

INVERTEBRATE

PHYLUM: Arthropods

CLASS: Arachnids

ORDER: Araneae

FAMILY: Lycosidae

GENUS: *Pardosa*

SPECIES: *coloradensis*

Thin-legged wolf spider
(coloradensis)

GLOSSARY

ARACHNIDS
The class of invertebrates that includes spiders, sun spiders, harvestmen, ticks, mites, scorpions, pseudoscorpions, whip spiders, and whip scorpions

ARTHROPODS
The phylum of invertebrates with exoskeletons and jointed legs; arthropods include arachnids, horseshoe crabs, insects, and myriapods

CAMOUFLAGE
The disguising of an animal by the way it is colored and patterned to blend or merge with its surroundings

CARNIVORE
An animal that eats other creatures

CHELICERAE
A pair of appendages on either side of an arachnid's mouth; many arachnids use their chelicerae for feeding

CRUSTACEAN
An invertebrate belonging to the class Crustacea; crustaceans include crabs, lobsters, and shrimp

EVOLUTION
The change in living things through time as they become better adapted or suited to their surroundings or environment

EXOSKELETON
The tough outer covering of an arthropod's body

HABITAT
A particular type of surroundings or environment where plants and animals live, such as a desert, mountainside, pond, or seashore

HOST
An animal on which a parasite lives and feeds

IMMOBILIZE
Make something unable to move

INVERTEBRATE
An animal without a backbone or spinal cord

LARVAE
Insects at a stage of development after an egg but before maturity; *larvae* is the plural of *larva*

LATIN
The language used by ancient Romans; scientists still use it to classify animals

MAMMAL
A warm-blooded vertebrate that feeds its young on milk and has hair or fur

MICROSCOPE
An instrument used to magnify the view of small objects many times

MYRIAPODS
The class of invertebrates that includes centipedes and millipedes; myriapod literally means "many legs"

OPISTHOSOMA
The back part of an arachnid's body, containing its heart, lungs, and reproductive organs; also called the abdomen

PARASITE
An animal that lives on or inside another animal, feeding on it while giving back nothing in return

PEDIPALPS
A pair of appendages possessed by all arachnids, located in front of the first pair of legs

PHEROMONES
Chemicals produced by an animal to attract a mate or otherwise affect the behavior of another animal of the same species

PROBOSCIS
A thin, tubular structure used for feeding by certain invertebrates

PROSOMA
The front part of an arachnid's body, bearing its mouthparts and legs

REPRODUCTION
The process by which a new generation of animals is created

SCAVENGING
Eating the remains of animals that died through natural causes or were killed by another animal

THORAX
The middle section of an insect's body, bearing its legs

VENOM
A liquid poison used to injure or kill prey

VERTEBRATE
An animal with a backbone and spinal cord

FURTHER RESOURCES

AT THE LIBRARY

Burnie, David. *Mini Beasts: The Microscopic World of Tiny Creatures.* New York: Dorling Kindersley, 2002.

Camper, Cathy. *Bugs Before Time: Prehistoric Insects and Their Relatives.* New York: Simon & Schuster Books for Young Readers, 2002.

Montgomery, Sy. *The Tarantula Scientist.* Boston: Houghton Mifflin, 2004.

Murawski, Darlyne A. *Spiders and Their Webs.* Washington, D.C.: National Geographic, 2004.

ON THE WEB

For more information on spiders and their relatives, use FactHound to track down Web sites related to this book.

1. Go to *www.facthound.com*
2. Type in a search word related to this book or this book ID: 0756512549
3. Click on the *Fetch It* button.

FactHound will find the best Web sites for you.

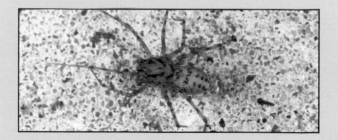

INDEX